THE OVERMIND

James Byrne is a poet, editor, translator and visual artist. He has published seven full collections, including *Of Breaking Glass* (Broken Sleep Books, 2022). A longtime teacher of poetry and transnational poetics, he has co-edited and co-translated several books, including Ro Mehrooz's *Poems Written Through Barbed-wire Fences*, a collection of Rohingya language poems, and Ashur Etwebi's *Five Scenes from a Failed Revolution*. A Selected Poems of his work is forthcoming in February 2025.

PRAISE for *The Overmind*

In *The Overmind,* I think we do 'enter the interlude', a between-place full of spectral distortions, subconscious stirrings, subterranean mutterings. It's a collection with a keen ear to the infrasound; it catches words half-heard, sees things slant through smoke or shadow.

Byrne's book is ghostly, in that it is populated by apparitions. It is also ghostly in that it enacts kind of portable haunting, a 'poltergeist among [the] living ghosts' of history, literature and contemporary culture. There's a playfulness at work here, a restless, tricksy engagement with traditions of art and forms of language, that's both spooky and disruptive.

There are those who exist on the periphery, whose music is made in the undersong. I think that's who this collection is for – the working-classes, the ghosts in the machine.

— Fran Lock

After reading *The Overmind,* you are immediately impressed by James Byrne's steely, yet tensile intelligence, and by the cognitive concentration he exerts on each poem, as though using a kind of pressure-valve syntax, which in each compressed statement feels as if it could burst and let seep, at any moment, the hiss of any still unused imagination. By imparting unremitting torque direct to every word and image, the poetic voice creates an immense repellent to any linguistic slack. Reason enough it seems to read this collection, for amid Byrne's subversion of the written word and the masterful way in which he keeps language in a state of (almost) aporetic equilibrium, the readers will realize, almost at once, that they are encountering one of the least ponderous minds in contemporary poetry, and one of its most Promethean voices.

— Paul Stubbs

ISBN: 978-1-916938-60-1

Cover designed by Aaron Kent

Edited and Typeset by Aaron Kent

Broken Sleep Books Ltd
PO BOX 102
Llandysul
SA44 9BG

Contents

The Overmind

James Byrne

Broken Sleep Books

For Gaia, who *is* everything

In memory of Niall McDevitt
and my brother, Robin

If I could visualise or describe the over-mind in my own case, I should say this: it seems to me that a cap is over my head, a cap of consciousness over my head, my forehead, affecting a little my eyes. Sometimes when I am in that state of consciousness, things about me appear slightly blurred as if seen underwater.
— H.D.

[T]he Overmind releases a million Godheads into action, each empowered to create its own world, each world capable of relation, communication and interplay with the others.
— Sri Aurobindo

Walk, in silence.
Don't walk away,
in silence.
— Joy Division

APPARITIONS

Enter the interlude, the shadowbox, the waltz.

Re-
verse your voice first, then wake up
plumping the pillow—

attunally sounded out like

crystal
cut
dust.

Cello funeraries. Burnt gristle on the hook.

Once, I saw your face inside a mirror,
looked back,
swallowed myself
in the glass.

Charcoal outhouse, rooms,
pyramids. Mells of history.

We never thought of being alone. It kept me
from overfeeding the boy under my skin.

Tomorrow, how will you know? I've had to wait
lifetimes. Tomorrow, the idea of it could change
my name into redemption, or break it into pieces.

Tomorrow as midnight and, by morning, wind-
sieved, sand into sun, a path to light the dunes.

Tomorrow, or else and unless the song leads me
waiting on a dark-windowed car to arrive, its tail
strewn with black ticker-tape. Tomorrow as breath

blown

out

(not yet).

How long left to wait? I've shaken hands
with myself so often I know the dry con
-tours, the underbones. Dread in the arc
of a question mark. You don't hear
something back like that and live un-
changed. It's not like one note is blue
when the echo is red, or what can be held
down by someone's idea of organic logic.

Same old friend,
same old sky—

I listen for you to enter
                the empty room
at night.

I turn up the music until it

stops.

THE OVERMIND

I was wearing a jellyfish over my head. I could barely see at all—
must have fallen down a basement aleph, bumping off the steps.

I imagine it was the same way I fell when my mother was pushed,
my foetus six months gestational inside her. The sting made my skin

feel like it was being flayed and when I opened my eyes, I saw
the walls shudder, as if mid-quake. I asked the doctor, what is

the distance between curse and symptom and she wrote out
her reply on a prescription pad: *it's like trying to measure the smell*

of death. June, the air thick as tar, a sixty foot truck came rolling off
Shore Drive onto 67th, smashing the side of the cab. I saw it all

in slow motion, wearing my jellyfish cape again, a tunnel of pixelated
shrapnel, the taxi driver's airbag an exploding green mushroom.

Someone groans. *Who are you?* Face pressed against the glass, blood
on the dash. *Turn off the ignition, turn it off,* then doing it myself, but

unable to pull him out. I emerged from the sky-tilted passenger side,
as if opening the escape hatch on a submarine, and jumped down.

A fireman mummified my hands, and we stared at the battered cab,
the driver cut from the windscreen before shock-vomiting onto the verge.

Glowing red and white in the ambulance light, a young medic said:
you were lucky, most people don't crawl out of those. I wanted to call

my daughter, Gaia, realising I could still hold her in my arms, see her grow. Thank you. It is October, I have returned the jellyfish to the sea.

You've been given another chance said the doctor (strange term for anyone on the brink of divorce). To survive, I must decomplexify everything:

no cigarettes, no meat, no wine, no love (not yet). It's too early to say how things are going. One day I might wake up and not feel the sting.

IMITARI

How does meaning get into the image? Where does it end? And if it ends, what is there beyond?
— *Roland Barthes*

1

What is the first thing you remember in this world?

> Being washed in tepid water,
> a tin can bath beside an open fire—

> > all the faces candled and watching
> > > through the darkness.

2

That I am merely an extension of yourself.
Mismatched. Precarious from the start.

> > What have I asked of you?
> > It is too much. Too much.

To imitate. To portray. To represent
an image like the memory of doubt.

> > Missense of abandonment.

> > A mare   bucks

> > in an empty
> > > > field.

3

My father's eyes, murky from the drugs (morphonic?).
In the photograph, he comes round slowly in the chair.

Is the image, asked Barthes, representation resurrected,
mythic and antipathetic to lived experience? I cannot see

beyond it. In Avoca, before the dementia set, a yellowing
photograph of a spruced-up cowshed, the family house

where my father jumped over hedges all the way home.
We carry the portrait, asking locals: 'do you know where

this is?' 'Over the hill', gestures a man, but when we arrive
it looks like another empty field. My father takes a bottle

from the back of the car and, standing in the absence of his
house, gulps the sting of it down. 'It was here, somewhere'.

In Bray, over dinner, he tells me who he is for the first and
last time. 'My earliest memory is being placed me on the steps

of a large country house to ask for money...for the auntie they
abused'. Cutlery scrapes at silence. 'It was around Christmas'.

The image of my father recomposes itself, stares out the window.
'I remember' he said, 'there was a light snow falling on the lamps'.

Coda

Imitari, resemblance of memory. I have been portrayed,
represented, as if this were the fair copy of a life.

The first thing I remember, I was sitting on the toilet,
and fell in, convinced I was to be flushed down the dark

mouth of the drain. I remember a hot pulse of lightning
thrashed inside my body, before the rescuing of hands.

But no, this is not the first thing I remember. There was
a sound first, or the scattering of a sound, like an image

trapped in a kaleidoscope before shaken loose. Sometimes
I hold it up to the sky and the glass around my brother

breaks.

EVA AT CLIVEDEN

Eva, in service at Cliveden. Chromatic, blue blood, the seed.

Your undersong in the drawing room gone quiet, your face

shocked at the grate, a hand upon your shoulder. Eva,

you were panning the embers, not downing the sheets.

And he made note of your aloneness, your ability to keep

close with silence. And he watched you like a beam for roadkill.

In tomorrow's newspapers, one of his daughters will marry the primeminister.

Lineage-hewn, embassic. Who could touch a man like that?

As the ambassador said to the banquet hall: green is the colour of fine lawns
and arsenic.

On the way back home, you tripped over your shoes. Red blood.

Eva, there must be a hundred steps from the garden to the river.

The hand lied as witness: the stallion bucked in the stable all night.

Eva, was the wind not listening? The wind is always listening.

Insist she be discrete and then be rid of her, they said.

The family tree. The severed bough. The blackened root.

There's nothing more that is to be done or said about it, they said.

And if you knew the child's name, you never spoke it. Eva,

great-great grandmother, tell me, who did this?

For six hundred pounds, you can stuff your mouth with venison and pretend you are the country friend of a lord.

In the library, where Astor drank bourbon alone, many variations of *Beautiful Britain*. Cucumber sandwiches crust-cut over Jubilee High Tea.

For six-hundred pounds a night, post-aspirational, free-as-you-can-pay-for-it. Inanities of third series Netflix. 'Oh, yeh, that was when it was good, right'?

Walk down the stairs in Gucci pyjamas and slippers. Artic char, chalkstream trout, raspberry soufflé. How much fine-dining unmemories a manor?

For six hundred pounds, you don't have to mix it with the groundsman or the dogwalkers.

In the library, *A History of the Black-Haired People*. Thumbed yellow over pipesmoke.

For six hundred pounds. Money washes its murder face.

Unscandaled, to begin a conversation with your abuser.

In the room you clean for (Lady) Katherine, a large bay window faces the rose garden, while the back window looks out over a pet cemetery.

Oh, Tibbles! His collared ghost patters through the pantry cat jamb as you flap loose an ironed pillowcase.

Tomorrow will not open for you like the pull of curtains.

In the drawing room, they play Fates, how much it would cost to make you disappear.

You end a letter to your husband: *Please believe me when I say everything will be okay*. Everything is not okay.

The Jessamay Bride's eyes fix on you like the burning of houses.

Scandaled, shaming the poor. *There will be no further talk or conversation*, she says.

If you could only hide a little better with your eyes like the butler does. If only this were a conversation of the poor. Hitch up the lady's corset

too tight, your face stung by her gloveless hand.

First, a five shilling note, accidently floating in the coal bucket. Every room

a crime scene waiting to be chalked. Speculatrix eyes

of the Jessamay, who would raze you, quick as a flash of lightning.

Over the fire grate, imperiously impervious and tied with a gold sash. A
single note.

Ten shillings, a dairy of milk, bread and pheasant and no more a week of
mutton.

All you have to do is slip the money inside your apron mantelet.

Close the door behind you and be who they want you to be, as darkness.

What is ash, if not time spent?   I will not sign the visitor's book.

What is the sun to make fire?   Tell me the names she would not

speak.

Who cuts the caesura of voice?   A bell rings above the stable.

Where do you live in silence?   In the silence of filthy hands.

Said to the footman, where's the hammer?

Said the baker: I would hammer their heads together.

Said the cook to the porter, if not us, nobody will take her.

Said nobody and never the cook to her master.

A butterfly house flutters with traps.

Ten shilling notes hoisted like flags above the fireplace, but what is surrender?

Given over, then hidden, like secrecy in the attic.

If a man finds a damsel that is a virgin, which is not betrothed, and lay hold on her, and lie with her, and they be found...

No-one finds him on the inside, except you.

Ten shillings stuck to a gold vase, to diamond-encrusted chandeliers. Fives between the banister, in the dust you swept and swept.

The music room is spotless, but for notes wrapped around a harp, ivory keys of the pianola.

All you have to do is slip the money inside your apron mantelet.

A dairy of milk, bread and pheasant and no more a week of mutton.

Close the door and walk on through the dark.

Child, born to a family who didn't read, you read
Jane Eyre at night by candle, or from a looking glass—
faces *specking the gloom*, footsteps outside your door.
(Father, is it you?). Scent of beer rot and sweat, sound
of rushing wings, the shock of a pulse beating your ears.
Can I come in and we'll finish our little story? Was it
something like this he said? Bessie echoes a decade.
If family turns you over, it's the poorhouse or *something*
bad might be permitted to come down the chimney and
fetch you away. You sit it out for hours in the red room,
keep quiet, whisper your prayers and everything will pass.
(Father, will this ever pass?). This him and him, this
constant taunt of money. Rochester severs the bookmark.
Something bad that happened is happening again. Tulip
tongues wag, as if willing a *moment's mutiny* to light
the morning pink, a low sunrise on the parterre,
where they watch you watching them with binoculars
from the Octagon Temple. Your hand brushes orangeries
of flame azaleas, knowing how every leaf would stir a tea
laced with poison. *Why could I never please?*, Jane asks
inside the glass. You who endured too much of other
people's pleasure, underline *Silence! This violence is...*
most repulsive (they are repulsive) and *Master! How is he*
my master? (nobody masters you). The word 'nobility',
a lie old as power itself, there's nothing honourable in it.
You had a job to do, this was all. Cleaning out the grates,
putting out fires, until flammable, a match ready to ignite.

Said to the rag n' bone man: enough nails for a coffin.

Said the ratcatcher: inside their coffins I'll find them.

Said the tosher to the mudlark, it was his dukedom.

Said nobody and nothing was ever asked of him.

I have a dream of setting fire to you and you go up in a great pile of money.

The fire kindles your sidewhiskers first, then your eyes, black to bubbling.

The foals from the stud come out
                    shrieking

                                    but there's no sound
                                    from their mouths.

And then the dream
          snaps shut
                    like in the gap before
                    waking up where

what you did to me was more real than anyone could think in real life.

                              Anyone but me.

I wake   daydreaming at the grates.

                    Twenty shillings

                              left by you
                              (if not you)

                                        at the hearth.

Richest man in England   oh noble savage   oh

                    to clean your house afire.

My great-great grandmother Eva walks past the Grand Avenue larch trees for the last time. Water in the Fountain of Love, pawprinted mud, the duke's hounds chasing squirrels at dawn. Why is it the rose garden wilts dry, as if its petals had been pressed in a book? She does not care for the question, looks straight ahead at the manor, once a fortress. A bag of nails rattles in her apron—poltergeist among living ghosts—a hammer raised in her hand and the seed of a child to raise in her stomach. *Nobody will believe you*, he said, *and the bastard will work the grates just like you* he said (and, yes, little Nora, she did). Slip the hammer inside your pinafore, its head-weight bearing against the umbilicus. Born of sin, of violation, but you must let the child live. The story of a father, an unknown soldier in the Boer War. This is what you will tell her. They never found him, he never came back. You walk through the servants entrance for the last time and begin at the southern terrace, dark with dawn shadow, the whole house still sleeping. Light the candelabra, to see what has been left overnight and every day for the past week; an envelope in the fire grate stuffed with shillings. *You would do well to take this*, he had said. And by god, you have taken it. With one blow of the hammer, you nail the envelope to the wall. Money, its failed spell, dangles from the partition. Enter the drawing room, another envelope, another nail in the wall and the manor wakes up amazed, the duke in his Ceylon robes, bustles down the staircase, the dogs going off, but you hear nothing. In the library, memory retches, his hand on your dress, pulling you down and further. You nail the envelope to the desk and, when he opens the door, enraged but hesitant, you raise the hammer again above your shoulder and shout *Back. Stay back!* Confusion of eyes, the dilemma of power to protect itself above everything, he steps back. *You, foul sir, would do well to take this.* Dignified and calm, you exit via the terrace—thick fog, steps to the garden, to the river, where the Thames appears to rise with smoke.

LOVERS BEACH

Plant a foot from the rickety boat
and wish for luck. A totem of rock
points to invisible stars, and the wind
grins, lifts an umbrella from the soft
stake you made in the ground.
To enter into this requires a little

burning of the skin. A man alone
in the water, his lover lounging
beside a tower of mango, sighing
to the sun. Just a little burning of the skin.
By dusk, the totem's shadow smothers
its tide. Hieroglyphs of heron's lime

and blood. When the last boat arrives,
you wade in, leap over the waves.

DIVORCE BEACH

NO PADDLING. You can't just
dip your feet in. Many people
die here. Even to reach the shore,
you might as well be breathalised
or take a hit from a ventilator.
Riptidally, your future awaits.

People have died here. Others
scroll back through their Whatsapp—
last seens of the ex/ex-to-be. Are you
still awake? Is it much too late now?
Cracked molar of rock. No-one else
but you and the breaker's fume.

A solitary red flag declares: BEYOND
THIS POINT, EVERYTHING IS RISK.

FRACTALISED, HOW DO WE PICK UP THE PIECES?
   for Toby Mercer

Good enemy, the self
snapping at type-
writer keys, dummy-
fastened with smoke.

A long night to sleep
alone in the coolyard,
buffeted by silence.
The wind starts up

like a bell to a bull.
How is it we are
born before skin,
like some magic trick

gasping into hope?
Inside the mirror, I
break shape, form, re-
form. I cannot be fixed.

IF YOU WOULD LIKE TO MAKE A COMMENT ON THE MONARCHY
for Kārlis Vērdiņš

1

If you would like to make a comment on the monarchy,
here's an easy-to-fill feedback form which will be placed
on a file called 'Surveillance'. No locking on, just locking up.
The trick, he said, is pretend kindness living a life in waiting
whilst building up the most powerful PR company in Europe,
its stratagem: a royal face on one of the tabloids every day.
The more you see us, the more you might accept. Locked
into the weeks of your life. Shall we count them? No matter,
it's just a rough figure. Any complaint will be taken seriously.

2

I was invited to Buckingham Palace. 'A Commonwealth of Poets'
they called it. The crown seal at my door made me think it was a letter
from the taxman. I declined and wrote in the *Morning Star* how,
in photographs, the poets were half-bowing, haemorrhoidally
unsure (but sure to be sold back the photo for £16, with a special offer
to buy more, because the grandchildren will have to see them ridiculoused).

The next week the daleks were invited.

Wrote of how the queen had applied for a state poverty fund
(anyone on the brink might apply). Her application was to heat
Buckingham Palace. In winter, the museum wing raised its charges.
When the energy bills spiked, the elderly froze in their homes.

The next week the daleks were invited.

3

Monarchy: the spider walking in our ears at night.
Outside the window, St Georges still wears the sign
of the Gorée. See the gate painted gold? It used to be
the king's procession route. Monarchy, hotbed of empire,
slavery's landlords and rent collectors. Off the coast
of Senegal (the real Gorée), ships couldn't make landfall
to cargo more slaves because the dock was already
too full with corpses. There is no reparation for this.
Kārlis, we can only imagine what it is like to be taken
elsewhere. It's not the same as how your man dreams
carefree in the public bath. The story in the newspaper
is of how the king employs someone to tie his shoelaces.
Another warms the white gown in which he sleeps.

AMERICANS TALKING ABOUT GUNS

Take away the gun, he said, and you
take away the history of this country.

The gun of this country pointed
at everyone—from neighbour

to State, at the head of my son. Inside
the gun of this country is another gun—

congress, filibuster, capital,
murder. The gun of this country

someone else's country— nations
who called it by other names: mothers

and gods. There's nothing more
relaxing than a morning on the range.

This AR15 shoots straight as a dime.
Every time. Hold it. The gun covered

with blood. I keep everything in this
rifle cabinet loaded. In case they come

at night. I pay attention. I know what's
out there. One day they're coming and

I'll be ready. This rifle is my temple.
It was my father's and his father's before,

and his too, down to the years it took
to *settle* this place. A bullet from that gun

ripped a hole clean through your British
flag. I pray to this gun. I talk to it, as if

talking to my ancestors and to you,
my protector. Father, son, holy spirit.

327 people shot every day in America.
Over a third shot and killed. Every day

23 children and teens, 6 dead. Every day.
As if you can't just act on the stats.

'My ten year old daughter could shoot a baby
deer' he said. 'Straight through the heart

from 30 yards. She's *that* good'. The figures
omit injuries caused by civil insurrection.

THE LAWYERS

1

I am not the kind of person that would ever ask to meet you.

Trouble at the funeral, you have arrived uninvited,
wearing a cold grey suit with a pocketwatch plumped
and a gunge-green handkerchief. You open the watch.

Time is running low, you say, *everyone must pay their price.*

So, what is my price?

2

A day after the accident, in a hotel room
in Manhattan, I picked another lawyer
first. 'I've been in a car crash' I said.
'What happened?' replied the lawyer.

'I don't know, I was already hunched over.
I think I was texting' I replied, and he hung up,
not thinking I might have been the passenger.
So I called you instead and now, months later,

you speak three sentences in a row beginning
'look', the same way Trump defended the obvious
bullshit on his campaign. There's only one thing
worse than a lawyer, a Republican lawyer.

'Look', you said before the retainer was signed:
'this one could have deep pockets'. And I shivered,
imagining how you've said this line over and over
again. Where do we stand? How many medical bills

do you want me to rack up? Yesterday on our call
(never in person, always Zoom), you were distracted,
looking at your phone five minutes in before taking
the inevitable call: 'Look, sorry, I've got to go'.

3

'This will only get worse', you say, flippantly rehearsed
and overplaying it like some vaudevillian actress. Letter

after letter writ and signed off with a squirty laugh
of fire. 'Inside of this, there's a little girl here' you say,

not knowing the first thing about her. The searching glance
of her eyes, the weight of tears, the questions she'll ask,

never sure if she's heard the right answer. Prosecution
or Defence, it doesn't really matter. Lawyer, lawyer,

your moon is a coin, your sun an instrument of torture.
Yes, there's a little girl here. You're speaking to her father.

OF DESIRE

I have written about this. A desire to communicate,
to obfuscate. Desire: transitive verb. What I want /
long for / crave is in a state of constant change.

I told you what I wanted but forgot to mention every-
thing else. How, desirous, I do not know what I want
and may not want what I know. How, fluxive, sometimes
I am thinking about Nietzsche, sometimes I am thinking
about boiling a kettle. My body is chemically different
in the morning than it is in the afternoon. Fissured,
polyvocal, cameo, transindividual, occasioned, multifocal.
I, I. Selving, cast into the inevitable shattering of the sea.
Where did you go? I am here, over here. I can't find you,
turn away from the light. Sometimes I want to call you.
I pick up the phone and tap out the numbers but hang up
before it dials through. What could we say to each other now?
All grown up and stretching out the limits of our childhood
skin. I didn't call. What with everything else we might say.
Desire to speak. To be given space: infinite requests
made against silence. I'm repeating myself. What might
yet nourish me is incomplete, intermittent, ever-shifting.

Let me start again...

I am left unfulfilled. Incapable of sustaining a fixed self,
therefore easily broken. Trying and failing to learn
the river's humility. Sometimes it's just the wind
making my eyes run, sometimes I walk in the woods
for a sure place to hide. These things may be seen to help,
but there is no cure. Desire, always residual with lust,

since language itself is erotic. I have written about this,
I have been saying these things for years. Whole days
lost inside my footsteps, trying to wake myself up
from myself. How to move in and out of stasis.
Simple acts of daily transformation. Perhaps I could
refine it better with hindsight, not overly pressurised
by the syllables inside my mouth. How I want to offend
my own basic literacy. I, a labourer's son carrying
plank rot and a bag of nails, a blundering detective
who cannot solve the clues to his own case. I demand
a fresh enquiry after the enquiry. I am unfulfilled.

Let me start again...

It's a kind of self-dentistry. I have written about this.
To be remade, or increasingly fractured. To recollect
the boy in the photograph. Always the crisis: to change
into something else. A tightening of skin around hard-
bitten nails. All I admit to is the writing of the writing.

[. . . . .]

My brother, living in the ellipsis, wrote the missing line.
In night whispers, in dreams, his body appears through
a blood-spotted sheet, a keyhole inside a golden dome,
where he announces himself as medicine. How am I
to take this? Desire unstopping, yet continuing to flow.
Brother, among banished mothers, diminished but yearning.
You were just a little boy who could not just reach out
and touch him. Shelves of Freud. Always the dead father.
I write to him, the wisher, the one whose desire was denied.
I've been thinking about this for years, but didn't speak up.

How what resurrects, refashions the dead. How I tried
to build a mosaic out of his absence. In the rest chapel,
I held his hand, blood-drained, and noticed how his eyes,
once so vivid, had sunken back into their skeleton. I
wanted to view him more starkly, as if more complete,
but turned away and wept onto the pages of scripture.
It only ends with us. Only in death is the end of desire.

ISOLATION

April foolery. A page torn from the morbidity report. Contact tracery over a new contract. Just kidding. In Fuller's idea of quarantine the pope merits paradise. Virus as in pus, emanation. Zip up your semi-permeable protein coat and wait on the terminology of what it means to be tested or super-spread against index reports. I am telling you all this in the strictest of non-confidence. See Miriam's phrasebook on contagion and communal living. Page 7: what you cannot see, the fomite exposures on your door. Addendum to footnote on page 14: Social distancing also meant where you could sit on Boston Common, on the Greyhound bus to Newark. And so on.

Outer body postured sideways. Distract yourself. A three-hour hunch and suddenly a paper moon lights up the room. Stock market effluvium. Yeah, the business is going to get a sock to the face alright. Easier to implode on remote. Voice against the rescue gate, plot bakes. And so on and so much for the holes in someone else's breathing. As if the wind blew open your mouth this aghast. Or Attila at the lectern might realise coma's more serious than money. Remoted. Dark blood through the tube repeats the joke's on us. You call and call, but cannot wake up the deepsleep.

Cuídate amigo. Cuídate. But nothing comes back. Closer to home and the business bee of friendship buzzes over an oeuvre. Time now to dust down my plans he says. As if writing relied on sure foundations. Ta for all that *stuff*. The act of consumption, feather to bone. Striven like a horse troop, and where does it get you? Death nearer known, slapped too hard on the back for coughing. Cough it up. Force yourself to look away from the window. A spider circles its web, eats the cocooned wasp. Vanity, forgive us this loneliness. All these barriers to song. Before summer comes, the entire sky will be pockmarked with perspiration.

Carnally hygienic. Zigzag past dog walkers texting from the leash. Subdolent. Quiet. The kind wind has nothing to do with. Blades shucked with dew. Sniff the living will against your muzzle. Beautiful world it was, hiding inside a mazework of tree bark. How to climb your branch, when nested so long? Fly up, bird. Tend to your mother's cracked femur. Board the plane with a doctor's note flailing from your left pocket. Rage, rage, as Dylan commanded his father. Addressee returned for the letterman who signs directions to the exit. Interstellar, light as darkness. Not yet. First, we stand this field. Wheat yet to spike the grasses.

Attempts at communal singing, as if this were what language is. Stuffed bears at the window. Angel bear. An orangutan flanked by pink hippopotami. The consolation note's opening line does not write itself. Easier to bear up like samphire against the weight of sea. Bunting's oaks grieve: *sad is spring to perpetuate*. Time's (un)matter. The tilled soil melts in your palm. A wood pigeon looks on, impervious. Two squirrels scuffle against a shelterless tree. Freeze-frame. What can you say to the she-grave veiling his face? That there may not be a country for the dead. Through low sun, I hear your thieving cackles, Mr Magpie. Click of starlings, a faulty telephone wire signals the cut line, the family omen.

[April 5th, 2020]

LONDON SYMPTOMS

1

A flexiflow line judders the cab. Mirror-
wince outside the steps of parliament.
Whisper 'survive' under my breath. I'm
not done with them yet. Text you waiting
with your parents at the rental. POSITIVE.
Union jacks line all the way from Trafalgar
to Regent. Whiteness blurred pink like that
onesie of Gaia's we let the colour run.
'Would you like to see her at the window?',
but you come out running and, something
like the last year, we miss one another in
passing. Try to hold myself in but, after
a minute, a wave, the image of her hand
ricochets from the window and she knows
something is off. Goodbye, not for long,
song of my life, your mother the melody.
I always thought we could fix anything.
Don't cry. Rest. Fluidic until morning.

2

Like a French hotel modernist in Paris
(say Montparnasse's Istria), I could get
used to this; croissant crabwise for break-
fast. But the headpound says otherwise
(otherwise what?) A surgically impersonal
room to soundproof the cough. A waiter
at the door by dinnertime, either scared or
dubious to see me semi-naked and masked

in my morning gown. 'Should I just sign
anywhere?' I ask, pen at the ready. 'No,
it's complimentary' he says, glove-handling
the tray at the base and backing away
with a speedy moonwalk. Muesli dust
catches the throat. My quarantine twin
hacks in solidarity down the hall. Nothing
to do but recline into a marshmallow duvet,
fronting off the tinnitus by writing to you
on your birthday, sleep until 12 'o clock.
The card: I'm sorry it couldn't be better
this year (the same you wrote to me
last Valentines). By morning, you and Gaia
waiting on the apex of Speaker's Corner.
Wrap the books in a sanitised tote bag.
Don't touch anything that might hurt you.

3

Enemy of Oxford Street and bodycarrying
what no-one wants to buy in the overheat.
Strangers eye suspiciously my protection.
At Blake's, off Bond Street, entitlement
harangues, a designer-clad man demands
from the shoe clerk why the street numbers
don't match up: 'Are the odds and the evens
all the same, or not?' As if it were simple,
like fitting up for a new pair of brogues.
Code red queues retained for exclusivity.
Try for coffee off Hyde Park, but a film crew
simulacras the entryway. A hammy actress
sipping cappuccino froth then powdering

her lips into a smile. Better to draw a curtain
on the afternoon and recover from all this
symptomatic stress of the privileged. Head
for the garden square, a private reserve
for billionaire residents. No point shouting
with a throat on fire, better keep mannered
as the puffed-up placards at Speakers.
Trudge back, footprint dust in the lobby,
quiz of eyes. *Goodnight. See you in the morning?*
Turn on the tv, turn it off again. The Tories
keep telling us to shut up about Rwanda.

4

Boneshivers. A final encore? The Nightnurse
knocked me out again. Awake at midnight,
percussive by mid-morning, cold-turkeying
from meds to see if the heat simmers down.
It's like concussion, but the punch withheld.
Tonight I should be onstage with my collaborator,
not wondering what to do with the last draft
I sent her. 'I hope you recover from the flu'
she said, asking for shredder edits (but didn't
Bansky do something like this?) and the image
of a pigeon painted green. Visions of drifting
up and down the back lanes of Conway Hall
to find the old Italian barber who trims
over a bottle of red wine (even at this time
in the morning). Mario, Luca, what was his
name? Loop back round Red Lion Square.
He's not there anymore and my hair looks
like a sideboard. Television friend a curse—

the Tory circus on Politics Live clowning up
the latest blameshift. Funny, how no-one
reports on the real Rwanda, why the flights
run aground. Kigali's clean streets spied on
by a 97% majority. There's no medicine for this.

5

Even the lord of ethics finds an exit.
We thank the honourable advisor for
keeping his mouth shut. Sussex Place
in the heatwave, and every other white
man looks like a rich kid displaced from
some boatcruise holiday. Capital England,
punishment served in the name of justice.
A cough that keeps gathering bile
and phlegm. As if any island might not
depend on global migration. 'Look
what they've done with Marble Arch.
It's blaady bootiful' says the suit n'boot.
No mention of Tyburn. Heads on sticks.
If you cut the principles of whiteness
open, its primary colour is blood. Odious
unethics. The idea of a country unioned
(Celt-censored), flying the gallows with its
Primarks made in the far away cruelty
of a Bangladeshi sweatshop. At Questions,
the croquet lawns must be heaving, barely
enough sitting for conversation, though
the question remains URGENT. 'We have
stan-daaards' says the minister in mock
Hiawatha-toned English. Oh. And you

think we haven't guessed at what they are.
Odious. Substandard. It's time to go.

6

Someone I cannot see is coming in a car
for you and Gaia. Pictures of her looking
confused as she tries to open the vast
emptiness of a kitchen drawer. Last night
when I stood steaming on the doorway
of Inverness Terrace (the posh pad
your parents rented), she waved at me
with a sadness I'd never seen before
(projection of my own at the window?).
Heart-gasp, losing breath until Leinster.
Someone is driving a car for you and
opening the door while I check out from
underneath the powerkeg and head
north. Distance of home so I might return
to you without this humming in my ear-
lobes. Outside the hotel, oaks shed pollen,
pigeons shelter on high branches,
preening themselves and dumbfound
with a shock at the swoosh of a street-
cleaner's brush. Tired yet meticulous,
he makes his round towards Seymour,
flaps open the mouth of a binliner,
and shakes his head at the ground.

7

If you could count between the cracks
of buddleia on the Merseyrail, levelling up
would mean trialling the front bench for—
where to start?—crimes against the people.
SECTION GAP reads the sign and the train
stalls twice before taking off with caution.
Gun graffiti at Sandhills. What's a glock
when the bullets are already loaded in them,
asks the boy, but no-one is able to answer.
Outlier platforms at Aintree jungle into
unweeded brush while going the other way
down the M6, lorryloads of kale and cavolo
nero for Sloane Square restaurants. Level
up. Level me this. Cessation petitionaries,
policies written in the North West, a reply
to Thatcher's hate memos: 'Dear Douglas:
'I want Liverpool off the map' she said.

WESTMINSTER ABBEY

Privilege like a prayer that choses who is
washed to order and who is washed unclean.
Show me his hands said the messenger,
and I'll show you the crime. *O viper, O man-*
drake. O memory of sin beseeched and stung
to life in the name of sacristy. A choirboy
sings for doves to fly from the canon's mouth
(not knowing that the barrel is loaded).

At Poet's Corner, Ben was buried upside down.
Someone always counts the donors, who pays
their debts before leaving, who doesn't. GLADSTONE
clutches his spear. PEEL pulls up his flabby robes.
O, this was what I feared. To be surrounded
by those who deny us the miraculous.

LUXEMBOURG
for Shehzar Doja

The Rue of the three glands obscures
Parc des Trois Glands—three acres

of luxury walking under Pafendall
streetlamps towards the Exhibition

of Skin. A tarantula wearing a Nazi hat.
You have returned from Dhaka, gut-raw,

staring down a plate of overripe kippers.
Your head is somewhere else, you say.

At the tram stop, cheese-grinning bankers,
Jock-like, slap each other on the back,

eyeing-up the company secretary
hard at the task of counting up

a bounty's worth of chocolate eggs.
The market is cracked. Wurzel cobble,

a riverine of water from a burst pipe
(how much needs to be lost before anyone

notices?) Anti-Samaritans in winter coats sleep
awake, sidestep the worker's flooded hands.

At night, they dream up new excuses,
how to leave us behind for other planets.

EMANATIONS
for Niall McDevitt (1967 –2022)

1

Who outstared Balor's giant eye in Connacht,
and lit the fire under Lugh in London, vatic
activist, walking the imagination of streets.

Whose megaphonic clarity blunts the scrapers
blocking out our sun like modern millstones,
who is rageously out *because life is outrageous.*

Top-buttoned at the gig with the absinthe bar,
here's a candle to light your way, another swig
from the glass to say thank you, sláinte, salud.

2

Family the wound. Your mother across the Irish sea and you
sent away like a wartime child. Exilic, to outman the old man's
jealousy, you sleep in the cave of a palindrome says legend—
Niall, who offered to kiss a 'loathly lady' for the sovereignty
of Ireland. The idea of unification in your name, the one good
scheme that might yet come from Brexit. Childhood hostage,
Torna, poet-druid, found you waiting inside a hungry gorge
and raised you among sages. At Syracuse, I catch your enemy
Eochaid on the runway, his cancerous Pictish arrow smothered
in silks of undercloud. Tomorrow, fretful but thankful, to see you
a last time on the Ladbroke Grove, resting in your open casket.
Eyes close for peace. Emanation: the Great Humanity Divine.

3

In the Blake interview you made, planting roots before Paradise,
a biblical phrase broke me down: *numbered, numbered, weighed
and divided.* Julie, in who your love was synergistic, aura-entire,
dresses you in suit and polka-dot Baudelairian scarf before I arrive
wondering how to walk the unmappable city without you. Redraw
the map you'd say. Steal a drop from Chaucer's parturial fountain,
fish out Shakespeare from his river digs; the innocuousness of a
London carpark explored excavationally, one of the city's holy sites
you said: *Will lived in here.* Arms stretched as if to channel fumes
of history. *Bay 18. His room right there beside that yellow Porsche.*
Mindwalk back to the nearest Wetherspoons. Someone over their
glazed roast and gold bar ale asks you your name. Niall, a torch
flame raised against Romano Britain, who fought the colonisers
of Leun Deun 400 years after Jesus first exodused in the desert.
Niall, you reply, smiling with *cheers* to touch the strangers glass.

4

If you were   here
                   you'd laugh

                        Blairstown next to
                        Buttzville

one thing   but

                        Blairstown next to
                        Hope

5

The bus drags into Manhattan, a sports apparel store off 26th. It's black/
white frontage mirrors your debut, *b/w*. Inverse of (W)illiam (B)lake,
Yeats. A boy ('Adam'), his torso gleaming on the ancient cinema screen of

Tamesis. Cartographic telepathy of the mental traveller.

In 2009, from Alphabet City, I sent an invitation and you delicately steered the subject, not mentioning Washington. There's a Crane walk waiting to happen, you said, but we never went there. At Hart's house in the West Village, flipping pages, lost at sidewalks until the spider lattice of Brooklyn Bridge, I fold down a line from 'Voyages':

Draw in your head and sleep the long way home.

6

In Tutuola's *Palm Wine Drinkard*, Drum drums to the sound of 50 drummers and Song sings 100.

Poets are better at numerology than mathematics. 100 is the temple, you said.

The poem, a singing temple. The song where Dance dances with The Father of the Gods Who Can do Anything in This World.

Bushwalk the jungle without eating for several days. Arrive exhausted at the scene. He (The Father of the Gods Who Can do Anything in This World) dances to the tune of a Half-Bodied Child with all the spirits of the forest.

This is where the ecstatic lives. *Out there, Cultic, weird.*

And so Dance dances and the song sails on air.

At the Tabernacle, John Crow reads 'The Drum' (your 'happiest poem'). His Goose steps in for the chorus (the whole poem as choric).

Happy, as in ecstatic, ex-statis. Singing out of/into the body.

This is where the imagination unhoods.

Drum and Singing and the Dance dances on with a kind of *spiritual scurrility*.

This is where the imagination flies. Above -ism, pure style.

Drum, words made by ear—of tympanum, of *Romme*, of *hum*.

You leave the Half-Bodied Child (who is also your child) behind and The Father
of the Gods Who Can Do Anything remembers to do something. His juju
fleshes a tree into the shape of a canoe where you slip away across the water.

Grief's village of skulls tap-tap the forest floor.

Drum inside a wraith of silence, singing—

> *And in all minds was hung a drum-skin of goat*
> *And in all hands was a witchdoctor's stick:*
> *Brotherhood of the bodhran,*
> *Sisterhood of the singing bowl*

7
Dinosauric I
scroll you
       August
       2017
              your last message—

how 'R4 didn't even mention Htein Lin'
the British Brainwashing Corporation
some aloof article about Vicky Bowman
in Insein.

Try and do something   /   We must do something.

Activist, until the final note
sent without reply in the middle of conversation
(language best held over for the live cut of meeting)

Lachrymose over Pastel de Nata and green tea
unembarrassed and yet unable
for the first time
not the last time (is this the last time?)
to drink your pint down.

Struggle to get you home (are you home?)
Pause at the rails, the bus shelter,
lean on the arch to ask:
what happens
if the soul cannot fight anymore?

Eternal Death.
In the Heavens of Albion
and Before the Gates, Enter
Jerusalem, the icon
of emanation

It is never the end of your soul

8
Up with the milk,
un-caffeinated, I
mistake squares —
Parnell for Fitzwilliam.

The Irish Writer's Centre
warps
into the Irish Racecourse Centre.

You're a plasma, not a plastic Paddy
you said, the last time we were here
in your old town, Dublin,
was it a decade or more?

Under the streetlamps of O'Connell,
I met your father, Michael—
a slim collection of Paula Meehan
peeping out his cordorouy pocket.

From boulevard-wide streets,
slick with afterain—
a seat of purple rock cress aubrieta,
solitude of a convent wall,
your mouth grinning in gaps
of rockface shale.

Sun flicker on the stain glass
windows of Earley Studios
on Camden Street Lower—
the little sisters of the Assumption
stand on the steps, satchels in hand
(where do they go if not ascending?).

The photograph mentions how
the building has been 'restored'—
Keavans Wetherspoon Hotel.

You'd insist we sit for a pint.
Toast to Keavan over the British
bastardisation (Kevin). An empty
glass on the table, to fill your cup
I would pull you out of the water
at Glendalough, converge rivers,
the echolalia of our fathers, mine,
Mr Byrne, as you called him, meeting
at my wedding. O bereft speeches.
Regret's lot, best friend, 'best man'.
Tonight, the premiere of your film
about Joyce's secret wedding. How
not to weep through the curtain?

Across the street, Devitt's bar,
CLOSED,

Across the road: your dinery:
JERUSALEM

        Jump   *into the safety-*

          net of angels

            into the winged air

Jerusalem Coda

To drink a vintage cask—Rocks of solid fire—

Azure tears shed cold—In Regions of Humanity—

Los's hand a red globe—All forms of cruelty—

Pillars of folded smoke—Mirrorbowl of sorrow—

Through the tongue's gate—Albion, behold—

Thy beauty—In London's opening streets—

From emanation to flight

AFTER A TORRENT

In your sackcloth loin robe, look up—
a raven's beak is delivering bread
above your head, as in Preti's St Paul.
Look up—hang your coat from a hook
on the wind's back, tilt your breath
to the sky and dream, primordially,
as if you knew how to fly through
pitchfork rain. Clouds pass inside
your blood quicker than the turning
of a key. Childhood spins: a carousel
rusted out among beech leaves.
You live on, morphologically, as if
by afterthought, wondering why time
is rarely dignified by acts of time-
less charity. Sunset's purple garter
breaks on yellow satin. Touch of hands
above a petroleum-skinned city.
Santiago, Paris, as you wish it—
every mix of colour defines the self
transfigured, every form imitational
essence. Brancusi's primal cry echoes
the tearing of light. Inhale to exhale.
Look up—a rabbit moon silhouettes
the coastal road over Celastun,
irradiating sorrow, condolence.
You live with all the unsayables
in your voice when saying goodbye.
You take the bread in your mouth,
and carry on with somewhere to get to.

IMBOLC ON CLIEVES HILL
for Jesse Hill

A farmer's knife, dew-shiny,
aberuncates the green head
of a cabbage, flashes a mirror
to the chucklesome magpie.

A far hill intersects Haskayne.
The field's sanctuary opens on Gaw,
its frayed edges fertiliser-scorched,
sunkissed, as if by neural rot.

Footprints fossilise mudflats,
lasso-shaped puddles all the way
to the vacant observatory house.
Stand a minute, stretch your arms,

burrow your eyes into the dark soil—
wind to the west from the Irish sea,
a feathery necktie, a shanty kissing
to lift the mist from the harbour.

Sing! it says, but the ancestral flute
tunes up fugue-solemn. Up the path,
a man dressed entirely in blue walks
commiserably, head bowed down,

pondering what good will happen.
He moves into the future, thinking
he might bear enough to live without
consolation. Brigid's head of flame

a burning wickerwork. Grasses revive
from mud, a pilot light of ecstatic renewal.
Close your eyes, listen on the air and hear
the turning breath of the Sabbats wheel.

KITESONGS

Try, as the kite that is flying
in parallax to its own shadow.
Tail dancing from the ground,
bridle into vapourtrail, its red
spars cut the sky blue and take
their course from the sea. Fly,
little ship. One day I'll teach you
how to float beneath the sun.

    *
*   *
  *
    *
      *
        *

Safedistanced, kiterunning
over the grade's edge, far off
to the little mountain house
that is yours, but never lived in.
Red cord in the left hand, blue
cord on the right, and the wind,
changeable as a politician,
chooses where we go.

          *
       *   *
       * *
          *
           *
            *

I live inside loops, pockets of air.
Forwards, backwards, sideways
giddy yet reliable to tension.
I keep low to the ground at first,
hovering in my diamond silhouette,
bowline strung up like a requiem.
Braced to sail the leading edge,
I hold on tight to the line.

TO GAIA

Wales to the Wirral. Finland to Iceland, a V of geese telegraph north over the Celtic gateway. Where are they going, you ask.

It is never a straight line. On a crinkled map, I look for you. Shadows in the hawthorn. stillness inside photographs. Where is north, you ask? The circuitry of the path from the village opens up, then spirals away. There is no levelling of the compass.

Sleepless, you oscillate on trains, London to Liverpool, talk of alternate weekends. I measure calendar windows, traffic bulletins, service station exits, leery platform crowds at the buffers. Too late for bedtime Jackanoria.

I lost my father at the same age. You cannot measure it. The echoes we made in carparks, dissonant across time. Autolycus playing hide-and-seek in the hills of Bohemia. It is not the same.

Last night I dreamt of flashfloods, fire. There was a ship that flew and you were wondering whether to board, but I knew you had to go. I was wiping your eyes, trying to zip you up inside a tent made for breathing.

When we sit down inside the visiting room at the care home, my father gets up. 'Please, sit down granddad' you say. He gets up, blank, then smiling, mumbling in riddles of unbreakable code. It is not the same. 'Sit down, granddad', you say and he holds your eye, a child smiling at a child.

Last night I dreamt we were both walking around a mountain, but kept missing each other.

In an hour, you'll be coming out of Hedgehog class in those draconian pinstripes. Two years old and in uniform. The path below my feet is muddy.

Footprints circle back on themselves. My father drinks up the unnameable purple liquid as I wait for the message to flash. *Yes. Saturday. Lime Street.* 'Are we going to where daddy works?'

Cross fingers, count magpies, tip a black fedora. Fear summoning the jinx. One for sorrow. Two for joy. In the video you giggle, in the photo, pondering, morose?

Come here. My arms, your home. Crib beside the old bed, breakfast predawn, bartering at your imaginary bakery made of toys and pillows. *Come here, angel.* You are the whole world in a holophrase.

Take this crow feather, tickle it across your neck. Tuck it inside your sleeve for luck.

The stones you picked still jingle in my pocket. The song trembles softly back into the water.

THISTLE
after H.D.

My spinal ball, my leaf-like
duplicity, hold it in your palm—

flower and weed, wing stem, bract
sting, pink floret, all the bad blood

that made me. Love, hold this idea
of love, hold this, hold this thistle.

MEDITATION ON MEDIATION

1

To think what is lost might yet be returned.

To think what is returned could be fixed
/ fixed up?

[think again]

No mediator can mediate this

Silence squeezed into

¶ nar- ¶
¶ row ¶
¶ hall- ¶
¶ ways¶

Where once it was the most natural thing
to place an arm
across
your shoulder

the window curtain rests
too close to bear,

the cut elm will not
survive
replanting.

2

Inroads, furrow lines
of my face.

Don't go.

I won't go.

Glaze   o-
                 ver
    in
        public.

Walk out the nursery door

                blob

                eyes

& drive, drive, open-mouthed, until the car asks if I need a break.

~~Yes, I could use a break.~~
you cannot break.

Stand up. Mountain pose. Functional over emails, contracts, disclosures—

        sign this.

                Here,   not here.

Coda

In the vacant chair of a generically cream room,
tomorrow's guest waits with a delicate finger
poised over her lips. *Shhhhh*, she says, *sleep*.

I arrive home. Memories in a glass jar.
Peek-a-boo forest. A mermaid inside
a box collecting dust.

There is no mediation for this.

IN SILENCE

1

There was a chill you could feel standing at the door.

        The house still exists, I've checked.

        It's there, where the path runs cold.

        Perhaps the whole building is possessed.

        I've knocked three times and heard nothing.

        It's like sound, but without the clothes on.

2

Keep waiting if you want, sooner
or later someone might hear you.

Last time I stood on the porch for
hours until the dusk rose. A light

from the man's room above came on
too loudly and the change seemed so

unwelcome. You can keep knocking,
sooner or later someone will let you in.

What was your name again? I'm sorry,
things are so prescient, I forget to listen.

3

When they are here
it can be as spoken—

mistakes mistaken
for granted. Do you

enjoy it, the quiet?

It is never quiet.

Statues on the wall like conduits.

When you were here
we might have spoken.

4

'Come down to my house.
Stick a stone in your mouth'.

Gossip, flint-sparked.

Open the grave and listen in—

the stone rolls back,
roaring.

5

Neither sorry nor grateful.

They call it

a pause. It is   not

a pause.

6

The difference between your voice and pindrops,
    like politics—

        once you're

            in
            there's
            no such
            thing as
            KEEPing
            OUT of it

7

WAIT   the sign above Kafka's typewriter.

Sensing his misfit luck, Gregor pulls up
a chair, reckons with a new idea—how
a single book might 'grieve for us'.

    [Withheld   breath   I

WAIT

    in the final decree   I

    grieve   for you]

        It's like the death of someone
        you love
            more than yourself.

8

Where

did you go?

I fell

into Puella's ear.

Where

did you go?

I am

falling

still.

9

It was a photograph I wished I'd taken. You
were twirling the yellow pannier of your dress
across a Hapsburg Ballroom. Laughing

without

making

a sound.

10

Ancient Greece tried to ban hope. They said
it could only lead to   disappointment.

But someone forgot to ask the farm girl
sweeping Dionysus' theatre—the boy
cleaning chariot wheels outside the gates

of the Parthenon.

11

At the doorframe, our voices pulse.

The years that took a life from us—

      is this all   we have

[. . . . .]

      to say?

                         [. . . . .]

12

Inside the door   the key's shadow

the aftersound   of your voice.

He said his wife gave birth to their inner child.

He said the world's water flows through a single tap.

He said Mercutio was a hothead in a quadrangle.

He said only fishermen sing the river's soliloquies.

He said he lives and dies by The Nether Lodge.

He said moonlight is the most imitated form of nature.

He said even the clouds are known for putting it on.

He said: who do you think you are, one of the three Brexiteers?

He said rainbones clattered in his father's voice.

He said his mother was from a rare breed of three-headed sabres.

He said the grandest lunacy is yet to come.

He said professionalism is the rife of doom.

He said Cyclops calls the sheep in from the fell.

He said Dryope speaks to him on the heath in mirror code.

He said Mountbatten believed in angel aviaries.

He said the wheat fields are cotted with blood.

He said he spoke loudest in bed.

He said the car waiting outside is the coffin.

He said it takes a shovel to dig the southern palace.

He said the worst kind of talk is blowpipe.

He said the best kind of nightmares are calligraphic.

He said blue is the most echoic colour.

He said television is the longest-running cartoon.

He said Trident is sharpening for Poseidon.

He said Galileo never took their word for it.

He said he always reads the parentheses first.

He said the Vatican got drunk on Maron's wine.

He said they believe in the official version of difference.

He said the wasp stores its last sting in the villages.

He said he was made to feel like a pigeon statue in an empty square.

He said all power is malarial.

He said foliage is really submarine.

He said to look out for the shadow curtain.

He said his name was Neminis, nobody among men.

IT WAS ONLY THE SCREECH OF AN OWL

You used to live here;
come in, shake off your boots,
take a look around. All
the pictures on the wall
were painted to welcome you
into the world before you were
born. Do you remember?

Come in, wipe your feet
from the big city. The man
in the picture wears red
straps over his heart, glued
to the canvas, a lock of hair.
His eyes, shocks of crystal,
measure a life inside a year.

It's just art, you joke, sardonic,
two years old and tickled to sleep.
Woken at the devil's hour—
the screech of an owl, firework
dreams lace the sheets. Sleep.
I am your father, your house.
I made all this to protect you.

THINGS YOU NO LONGER SEE

after 'Photie Man', Tom Woods

Jukebox tracklist (foxed paper). A man with a cigarette tucked behind his ear. In bird-winged cape, the selenium lights up his face.

A girl carries a Benson & Hedges tray through a hallway of backglancing fathers. What are you looking at?

A woman in red shoes, groceries either arm, right foot stepping into a pyre of fishguts.

Abruzzi shits the stoop. Alan in Gráinne, pensive as the bull's hide he stands upon. Miss New Brighton bronzes a c-type bonnet. His tongue rolls upper gums at the Wig Centre foyer.

Furcoatsisters, Adam's ants. The flashlit strop of the park. Dicky John's ghettoblaster. Tailspin to bodypop. Two mop-haired toddlers sleep in a Silver Cross, refuse bags for pillows.

THEY THAT GO DOWN TO THE SEA IN SHIPS AND HAVE THEIR BUSINESS IN GREAT WATERS. A whole morning left to play Peppy the Clown.

PAINT. ARTEX. Kirkby's uncladded risers smeared through tag glass. SPLIFFO. CSO96.

SEACOMBE	PAULA	SO
FAIRY	IS	IS
BOY	A WHORE	PLONKY

Trigger hand on the till. Unseen apertures of the gyratory. Dockers with arms folded at the Laird shipyard. This is your union.

Beach matt bamboo green-frilled at the Halio snack bar. Thatcher's tomb crates. Grandmother's hands bound in gauze mittens.

CHEE'S BURGE. JUMBO SAUS. Burgermouth stacks grin from the grills.

Over the reclining chair, a nurse administers the medication by pinching the patient's eyes open.

Fluke's Kingdom. A man in polished heels makes his exit.

PLUMS

I have eaten
the plums
that were in
the icebox
 —William Carlos Williams, 'This Is Just To Say'

Jay sits stoutish   though there is no place to sit.

I have eaten all the furniture.

So minacious. So bold. So Eton. So plum.

This is just to say . . .   joys shit sits Uta.

...And they were temporomandibular,
...And they were psychoforay.

Is Josi shut tasty?
Josi ssh sui tatty.

His joy sit status turns the camera turns on you.

Forgive me,

you were probably saving.

For breakfast,

I have smorgasboarded your war and published it in a black deathbox.

And which so sweet. Hast its joys situ?

Probably. Just Oasis shitty.

Beyond pisseries of cow parsley, beaten lumps,

<Hiya! It joust SSTS.
Justitia shy toss.>

the doctor bears his refridgerating hand.

   This is just to say...

     but my father abandons
     the sentence—

I'm sorry, it's like

     something eats away at me

       but I can't

    see it.

   And I can't

      kill it

   until

        it

     kills me.

Who could say this if not you? What is not justly said.

    Plum lumps.

    So cruel, so malicious.

What is the sentence?   I cannot remember the sentence.

[..]

What is the word?   [................]   I've forgotten the word.

Are you trying to say goodbye?

Yes, that's exactly what I was

trying to say.

SHEILA AND THE HARDMAN
for P.T. Byrne

1

Between Sheila—your first love—
who ran off with the postman
and 'the hardman' of the ward,
the bruiser lifting his belt strap.
(How could anyone harm you
like this? Grabbing at my socks,
hallucinating teacups, smoking
invisible cigarettes (you gave up)).
The big man came for you at night,
you said, brutish and bovine arms
still swinging. Father, is this what
happened?...'Yes, yes he was. But
Sheila was in love with me before
the football player. No, referee.'

2

Say something else so that we might
find him. Your sentinels cut down
too soon. The surety of a sentence
held by tethered string. Iris light
slips the curtain, so I close them—
blue stones of eyes, blackening
above a distant bowl of clouds. You
turn away, a series of snailtracks—
'She. She-la. She-la. Sheila. La-la-la.
Sheila. She was in love with him.'
Father, look at us in the mirror,
Seared back to the wick. Bovine?
Please tell me what you mean.
Father, again, just give me a name.

YOUR SHADOW KNOWS ONLY CONSTRAINT

A street remapped—
psychogeographics and single malt. Houses
shapeshift into those off the Common near
Berryman's exedra bench where the snow
pours in.

Though this is/will never be Boston, teenage
then, could you have gotten away with it?
(probably, yes).

Playing truant after bed and jumping
like your cat, Loris,
fence   to fence
at night.

Closing the door,
your shadow knows
only constraint.

Nocturnes
dry up cloudscapes, fill
the river's silver canvas—

all that measled light in the sky
around an open-mouthed moon.

RENÉ IN THE GRAPES
for Robert Sheppard

tension and intention
a face without a face

who would not scarce
himself from himself
is no sunnyside thinking
egg of the rooster

in mirrors,
pleating the gold bar,
similis out-apes
the human ape

fold spectacles
in a top pocket
skirr mausoleas
of water—

a seahorse draws waves
a boy invents ships
from shadow and stone

is this him? The other
voices the voice that speaks

the sandfaced man
wheezes with
cigarette laughter

confirms nothing
shuts his eyes
but does not

blink

PARADISE STREET
for Chris & Pascal & Sarah Ellen Byrne

A friend psychohistoricises
how sexually-transmitted
diseases once lived inside
a museum curated behind
this bus station, vanishing
at its sexual peak.

Walk through the lube
of invisible walls, past
syphilitic vitrines, exiting
the museum door onto
Paradise Street where
sailors clutched the gates
for ordinance, safe passage.

Above us, the unwritten city
records how the poet
Gerard Manley Hopkins
was unrooted by Liverpool,
stock-still outside the museum,
waiting for a bus to the future—
Hopkins, thin, young, a sexless
virgin in his robes, a genius
in the offing, yes, but
blasphemous to any Scouser;
to talk the city down
in your letters as 'museless',
what a useless cold lie
of a thing to say.

Hopkins: look in and out
of the water, the Pool's
reflection, nervewires vibrating
from the Mersey source. Perfect-
pitch you had, tuning-forks
for ears, unreceiving the city
that sang (three times) of love.
Across the street, Jung's dream
as direct transmission, Liverpool:
'that which makes to live',
activated at night, travelling
in its song, amusing to some, but
cloistered to the protomodernist /
Victorian, god-lost at the dock.

Hopkins, unmanned, unkind
as fourteen years of the Tories.
Your muse forgets to look
for itself here, lonely along the banks
at Waterloo, happier in suburbia—
Lydiate, Town Green, waiting
on doubt inside the station
waiting room, listening to winter
storms whistle under the door.
Your muse shipwrecked, adrift
from floating on the 'Pool of life',
unknowing what the city knows,
that we must change to survive.

Androgynine Celtic electrolight,
uncontainable by any hierarch.
The headlines read the same thing:

Tories out. Landslide majority.
Twilight reclaiming football-
quiet streets, an afterparty quick
as the turning of a road. Red walls
rebuilt, extra time won, the city
briefly changing its clothes—
costumes for the late night dress-up.
Concert Square curios walk the mile,
everyone but the bride wearing
black, cat burglars with names
on gold sashes made to look
like money, the bride smiles,
her mouth a ship lit with sun.
Geordie stags, Belfast hen-heels
clipping towards bouncered doors
of Mathew Street. History in the lines,
sleeping inside hyphens, those who were
born here and the others passing through.
A Liverpolitan, I pitch-pint in, the wish
to live communal as a union. Dinesh,
his utopic vision of a one-world city.
Liverpool, the first black community
in Europe, but the karaoke machine
jams on the chorus, docks formed
by slavery waves, proximal points,
hellships counted as human cargo.

Through the green gates of Paradise,
the muse evades her museum,
henchmen sing in a patchwork of masts,
a working chaos of goodbyes,
arrivals, fishing boats from Wales,

ice-frigates thawing from Norway,
ghost ships from the Caribbean,
gifts sent boxed up from London,
through a tapestry of nets.
With its hollyhock eye,
the distant lighthouse ushers in
a single ferry from Dublin—
chapters of a life vesselised,
yet to be written, but already
moving towards my unborn body
like smoke breathed in secret.

Sit still, she says. Straightens
the ends of an Irish silk dress,
and considers what to do, how
to climb from the rocking boat,
my grandmother, steadying up,
shushing her three children,
one underarm, my father, gas-
blue eyes yet to turn on full heat.
Come along boys, an unknown
man helps her with everything
that would fit inside a wooden box.

How to slither along the gangplank
when the waves slosh about like this?
Assimilate, side-to-side with the life
you had along with this opening
of a new life? Kaleidoscopes turn
the absent image—her husband,
my grandfather, across the Irish sea.
He shuts off the radio, the Trouble,

to which he is already too close.
In his chair beside the fire, a pipe
heaped with ash, he waits on news.

In the quiet darkness, what
must he say to himself? It is
not enough to know of hard time.
His wife left to look for work,
sending back money, sometimes
letters. *It's tough, love, I'm working*
three jobs. We all await you. Love, N.

My father at Milton's cottage,
nappy-towelled, gurgling beneath
his mother cleaning shelf ladders,
a mystery of books. It was the job
she enjoyed the most, the house
now a museum for Milton.
My father, a man old too soon
in his 70s, doddering with dementia,
toddler-like at best in the care home,
as he was back then, seeking Paradise,
regained, lost, regained, lost and so on,
learning what he will know one day
and every day now, how it is to forget,
snatching at fragments of a world.
Ancestral laundry in a high wind.

[....] [....] [....] [....] [....] [....] [....]

A hand at the landing gate,
beekeeper-delicate, holds on

to the box that holds everything.
On the train here, I rode backwards,
as my father does, but better able
to hold onto the story of a minute,
an hour flashing past, as if for him,
unable to unmanage himself.

The return train is late. Loop
round to Moorfields, listen in,
with my accent of southern,
nomadia, thankful to a decade called
home. Streets swell in the echochamber
of my grandmother, who boarded here
and knew what to do, the Liverbird
her spirit animal and guardian—
a gold icon at the gates of paradise.
For this, and for her to die in peace,
she must save, service to service,
the fortunes of a broken family.

Grandmother, I never met you.
You arrived at Paradise Street,
too soon, too late, your last words,
written of my father: *Tell Patrick
I love him. His dinner is in the oven.*

[....] [....] [....] [....] [....] [....] [....]

We say goodnight after toasting
to those who left under archways,
tunnels, muses and museums.
Not so much a hug of farewell,

more like poetics, permission
to continue. My friends convince
themselves into a whisky nightcap,
an alchemically-induced bar
that opens from a blank door.
Apprentice to mental travel,
the circuit rush of Bold Street,
the shadow-work of the Brow—
a cauldron of water swirls
off the dock and, from its rails,
I peer over the edge of history,
where someone held out a hand
to my grandmother and said:
please, can I help you ashore?

A FACE BORN OUT OF SUNRISE

Blot out time, keep fingers quick.
Blow the underdust from my sleeve and
live outside the silence we cannot say.

*

You stare into streetlights and ask:
Da-Da, is that the moon over your head?
Pull the door and the reception cuts.
Thud of heat pipes, the hum, the white
dispiritedness of the fridge. Here,
under the nightlamp and teething,
she rocked to dub in my arms.

*

Take Vasana before breakfast. Top
the bed with a blanket from her crib.
Misted crypt of a dream. Labyrinth
encounter of lost scent. Deadends.

*

I wake:
a goose feather has fallen (for luck?)
on the pages of your book. In the photo,
a face so bright it must have been born
out of sunrise. Tomorrow, we travel
to the same destination on separate trains.
You arrive home to the new room,
laughter like vertical ascent.

NOTES AND ACKNOWLEDGEMENTS

'Apparitions': the italicised section is from a track by Northwest entitled 'Same Old Sky' on their self-titled, debut album (2017). The poem is an automative, psychoacoustic response to the whole album.

The Overmind is indebted to various poetics and poetic thought, not least H.D.'s ideas expressed in 'Notes on Thought and Vision', republished in *Visions and Ecstasies: Selected Essays* (2019) which originates the term and my title poem. 'Thistle' is also inspired by this modernist poetics text. The title poem mentions an 'aelph', inspired by the end of Jorge Luis Borges' short story, 'The Aelph'.

'Imitari': the quote from Roland Barthes comes from an essay called 'Rhetoric of the Image' (1977).

In part 7, 'Eva at Cliveden' includes a quote from Dueteronomy. Part 8 features several quotes from the opening of *Jane Eyre*. The original grounds of the manor are now an exclusive hotel and National Trust site.

'Lovers Beach' and 'Divorce Beach' are beaches in the Bahia region of Mexico.

'If you would like to make a comment on the monarchy' was originally written as part of a collaboration with Kārlis Vērdiņš, performed at the Open Eye Gallery, Liverpool, on May 11th, 2023.

'Of Desire': parts of this text have been collaged and extended from a poetics written for my PhD, 'A Poetics of Desire' (2019).

'Isolation' includes a line from Basil Bunting, 'sad is spring to perpetuate' ('Briggflatts').

'Emanations' includes various quotes from Niall McDevitt, particularly his poem 'The Drum', published in *b/w* (see part 6). This section also includes quotes from Amos Tutuola's *Palm Wine Drinkard* and, elsewhere, further references are made to Hart Crane's 'Voyages' poem and William Blake's 'Jerusalem'. Niall McDevitt was a London-Irish poet, musician, 'walking artist' and actor. The poem contains some excerpts from conversations between McDevitt and the author.

'In Silence' includes a quote from the Garbage song 'Supervixen' (1995) and Franz Kafka's *The Trial*.

'Things you no longer see' is a collagic response to an exhibition of Tom Wood (a.k.a 'Photie Man') at the Walker Gallery in Liverpool, September 2023.

'Plums' was commissioned for *The Plum Review*, an anthology of responses to William Carlos Williams' poem, 'This is Just to Say', published by Broken Sleep Books in September 2022. This poem includes a series of anagrams to William Carlos Williams' line 'This is just to say...'.

'René in The Grapes' was written for and published in *An Educated Desire, for Robert Sheppard, at 60* (KFS, 2018). The 'René' referred to is (a doppelgänger of?) fictional Belgian author, René Van Valckenborch, an invention of Sheppard's, found in *A Translated Man*, published by Shearsman (2013). The Grapes is a pub in Liverpool.

'Paradise Street' was written after an evening in Liverpool with Chris McCabe and Pascal O'Loughlin. It makes mention of Niall McDevitt's term 'mental traveller' and Iain Sinclair's 'Liverpolitan'. Levi Tafari and Dinesh Allirajah are also mentioned. The early part of the poem is a critque of Gerard Manley Hopkins who said that 'Liverpool is of all places the most museless'. This poem is written for my grandmother Sarah Byrne (aka 'Nellie').

Thanks to the editors of various magazines who published earlier drafts of some of these poems. Particular gratitude to Aaron Kent at Broken Sleep Books for believing in and encouraging the work, for his considerable editorial eye (and ear). I always appreciate our discussions about poetics and poems and more. Thanks also to Emma.

Thanks to Sandeep, for the life we share through our daughter, Gaia (who this book is dedicated to).

Thanks to the communal support, conversation and connection with friends during the writing of these poems. Among others, I acknowledge Alison Trower, Chris McCabe, Niall McDevitt, Julie Goldsmith, Golan Hagi, Valzhyna Mort, Ishion Hutchinson, David Peimer, Ro Mehrooz, Stuart McPherson, Paul Stubbs, Robert Sheppard, Jesse Hill and Toby Mercer. Thanks to Forrest Gander for mentioning Sri Aurobindo's philosophy. As well as the teachings of Aurobindo and H.D., I also acknowledge H.H. and many unmentioned but supportive friends

LAY OUT YOUR UNREST

www.ingramcontent.com/pod-product-compliance
Lightning Source LLC
Chambersburg PA
CBHW020210090426

42734CB00008B/1008